cyber sign-offs

by

Hugh Murr & Sid Nigtures

for

Zak, Lydia, Oscar & Edward

(Our biggest fans & harshest critics!)

First Published in 2008

Paperback ISBN 1904312497
ISBN 13 - 9781904312499
Published in the UK by MX Publishing
335 Princess Park Manor, Royal Drive, London N11 3GX

contents

re: economy

| **From:** | Mark Mitchell | **To:** | Bob Gibson |
| **Sent:** | 18 January 2008 09:01 | **Subject:** | Re: Economy |

Hi, I think I've won the big one!

Yours

Jack Pott

| **From:** | Bob Gibson | **To:** | Mark Mitchell |
| **Sent:** | 18 January 2008 09:03 | **Subject:** | Re: Economy |

Nice one Jack. I'm struggling to make ends meet.

Yours

Penny Pincher

| **From:** | Mark Mitchell | **To:** | Bob Gibson |
| **Sent:** | 18 January 2008 09:21 | **Subject:** | Re: Economy |

You're right, times are hard. No idea what's round the corner.

Yours

Ian Flation

| **From:** | Bob Gibson | **To:** | Mark Mitchell |
| **Sent:** | 18 January 2008 09:24 | **Subject:** | Re: Economy |

Whatever you do don't take up gambling. It's a mug's game and you won't win.

Mark Mywords

From:	Mark Mitchell	To:	Bob Gibson
Sent:	18 January 2008 09:29	Subject:	Re: Economy

I know. Many of my relations way back in history lost the family fortunes that way.

Yours

Anne Cestors

From:	Bob Gibson	To:	Mark Mitchell
Sent:	18 January 2008 09:31	Subject:	Re: Economy

Sorry to hear that Anne – I must admit I've had a few bets on the horses recently.

Ray Sing

From:	Mark Mitchell	To:	Bob Gibson
Sent:	18 January 2008 10:25	Subject:	Re: Economy

Well don't knock it Ray – I won a huge amount of money yesterday.

Laurie Load

From:	Bob Gibson	To:	Mark Mitchell
Sent:	18 January 2008 10:44	Subject:	Re: Economy

I won some money at the snooker club last week.

Yours

Billy Ards

From:	Mark Mitchell	To:	Bob Gibson
Sent:	18 January 2008 11:03	Subject:	Re: Economy

Keep it to yourself Bill – you don't want everyone knowing that you're rich.
Anne Onnimuss

From:	Bob Gibson	To:	Mark Mitchell
Sent:	18 January 2008 11:06	Subject:	Re: Economy

Too late for that Anne – I've been spotted in the South of France
Monty Carlo

From:	Mark Mitchell	To:	Bob Gibson
Sent:	18 January 2008 11:11	Subject:	Re: Economy

Oh Monty – you need to take more care. My brother's just taken up gambling and I'm keen to see how he gets on in the coming weeks.
William Ass-Millions

re: drinking

| **From:** | Mark Mitchell | **To:** | Bob Gibson |
| **Sent:** | 21 January 2008 15:14 | **Subject:** | Re: Drinking |

I love a chilled drink in the summer.

Rose Hay-Wine

| **From:** | Bob Gibson | **To:** | Mark Mitchell |
| **Sent:** | 21 January 2008 15:21 | **Subject:** | Re: Drinking |

I prefer a spirit & mixer myself Rose.

Yours

Jim N. Tonic

| **From:** | Mark Mitchell | **To:** | Bob Gibson |
| **Sent:** | 21 January 2008 15:27 | **Subject:** | Re: Drinking |

Avoid cheap wine though, whatever you do.

Lee Frowmilch

| **From:** | Bob Gibson | **To:** | Mark Mitchell |
| **Sent:** | 21 January 2008 15:33 | **Subject:** | Re: Drinking |

I will Lee – I prefer the stronger stuff anyway.

Stella

From:	Mark Mitchell	To:	Bob Gibson
Sent:	21 January 2008 15:35	Subject:	Re: Drinking

Oh really! I'll drink whatever's available.

Al Cohol

From:	Bob Gibson	To:	Mark Mitchell
Sent:	21 January 2008 15:41	Subject:	Re: Drinking

So will I son.

Al Copop

From:	Mark Mitchell	To:	Bob Gibson
Sent:	21 January 2008 15:44	Subject:	Re: Drinking

I'm considering giving up altogether.

T. Total

From:	Bob Gibson	To:	Mark Mitchell
Sent:	21 January 2008 15:51	Subject:	Re: Drinking

I'm with you Mr. Total – I'll probably drink more coffee instead.

S. Presso

From:	Mark Mitchell	To:	Bob Gibson
Sent:	21 January 2008 16:01	Subject:	Re: Drinking

I prefer my coffee with milk.

Yours

Cathy Lartay

From:	Bob Gibson	To:	Mark Mitchell
Sent:	21 January 2008 16:11	Subject:	Re: Drinking

I've discovered drinking mine French-style.

Kath Etierre

.

From:	Mark Mitchell	To:	Bob Gibson
Sent:	21 January 2008 16:14	Subject:	Re: Drinking

Sorry girls, but I find all that coffee keeps me awake at night.

Yours

Dee Kafinated

From:	Bob Gibson	To:	Mark Mitchell
Sent:	21 January 2008 16:16	Subject:	Re: Drinking

I stopped drinking wine after a friend brought home of bottle of red from Eastern Europe.

Vinnie Gerr

From:	Mark Mitchell	To:	Bob Gibson
Sent:	21 January 2008 16:19	Subject:	Re: Drinking

You should stick to the finer things in life.

Earl Grey

From:	Bob Gibson	To:	Mark Mitchell
Sent:	21 January 2008 16:23	Subject:	Re: Drinking

I'm not so sure Earl. I've just acquired a couple of bags of apples and I'm planning on producing my own little tipple.

Bruce Ida

From:	Mark Mitchell	To:	Bob Gibson
Sent:	21 January 2008 16:44	Subject:	Re: Drinking

Let me know when the first batch is ready Bruce and we'll all get together.

Sally Brate

re: truth

From:	Mark Mitchell	**To:**	Bob Gibson
Sent:	06 February 2008 11:58	**Subject:**	Re: Race

We've got lots of Europeans moving into the village – I'm not happy about it.

Rachael Prejudice

From:	Bob Gibson	**To:**	Mark Mitchell
Sent:	06 February 2008 12:05	**Subject:**	Re: Race

If I were you I'd welcome them with open arms. Maybe throw a fete and have a lucky dip.

Yours

Tom Bola

From:	Mark Mitchell	**To:**	Bob Gibson
Sent:	06 February 2008 12:22	**Subject:**	Re: Race

Tom – you're a genius. I'm all for rewarding people who deserve it.

Sir Tiff E. Catt

From:	Bob Gibson	**To:**	Mark Mitchell
Sent:	06 February 2008 12:27	**Subject:**	Re: Race

Nice one Tiff. Are you sure they deserve rewarding or have they actually been lying? Only one way to find out...

Yours

Poly Graph

From:	Mark Mitchell	To:	Bob Gibson
Sent:	06 February 2008 12:33	Subject:	Re: Race

Good idea, although I won't be happy if you've been lying – you'll be punished.

Tanya Hide

re: curry

From:	Mark Mitchell	To:	Bob Gibson
Sent:	12 February 2008 08:14	Subject:	Re: Curry

Hi, thinking of having a curry tonight and I might really push the boat out and have a starter.

Yours

Sam Mosa

From:	Bob Gibson	To:	Mark Mitchell
Sent:	12 February 2008 08:17	Subject:	Re: Curry

Nice one Sam. Make sure you have something to accompany your main meal too.

P. Low-Rice

From:	Mark Mitchell	To:	Bob Gibson
Sent:	12 February 2008 08:21	Subject:	Re: Curry

You're on form Mr. Low-Rice. I was actually planning a simple salad.

Yours

Q. Cumber

From:	Bob Gibson	To:	Mark Mitchell
Sent:	12 February 2008 08:23	Subject:	Re: Curry

A belter Q – there's no end of choice at an Indian restaurant.

Dan Sack

From:	Mark Mitchell	**To:**	Bob Gibson
Sent:	12 February 2008 08:43	**Subject:**	Re: Curry

I know Dan. I took the kids for an Indian meal last week. They loved the big crisps you get as starters.

Yours

Papa Dom

From:	Bob Gibson	**To:**	Mark Mitchell
Sent:	12 February 2008 08:58	**Subject:**	Re: Curry

I always make sure my dad's mum brings something to go with my curries.

Nan Bread

From:	Mark Mitchell	**To:**	Bob Gibson
Sent:	12 February 2008 09:02	**Subject:**	Re: Curry

All this talk of food's making my mouth water.

Yours

Sally Vate

From:	Bob Gibson	**To:**	Mark Mitchell
Sent:	12 February 2008 09:07	**Subject:**	Re: Curry

Well make sure you don't dehydrate.

Walt Err

From:	Mark Mitchell	To:	Bob Gibson
Sent:	12 February 2008 09:11	Subject:	Re: Curry

I'm beginning to go off the idea of curry now.

Pete Tsar-Hut

From:	Bob Gibson	To:	Mark Mitchell
Sent:	12 February 2008 09:20	Subject:	Re: Curry

Me too – although I still want a takeaway.

Chip Shop

From:	Mark Mitchell	To:	Bob Gibson
Sent:	12 February 2008 09:24	Subject:	Re: Curry

Hey Chip – you should try the thinner cut versions – we call 'em crisps and they come in a very noisy bag.

Russell

From:	Bob Gibson	To:	Mark Mitchell
Sent:	12 February 2008 09:31	Subject:	Re: Curry

I can vouch for how tasty crisps are Russell – and they're less than half the price of proper chips.

Val You

From:	Mark Mitchell	To:	Bob Gibson
Sent:	12 February 2008 09:34	Subject:	Re: Curry

You can keep your restaurants. I love a night in front of the TV with a takeaway, watching the soaps.

Emma Dale

From:	Bob Gibson	To:	Mark Mitchell
Sent:	12 February 2008 09:38	Subject:	Re: Curry

Absolutely. I'd rather watch soaps than win the lottery.

Ed Case

From:	Mark Mitchell	To:	Bob Gibson
Sent:	12 February 2008 09:43	Subject:	Re: Curry

A couple of slices of hot buttered toast always go down well when I'm watching TV.

Yours

Kerry Gold

From:	Bob Gibson	To:	Mark Mitchell
Sent:	12 February 2008 09:48	Subject:	Re: Curry

Why not ask your mum if she'd put some spread on as well?

Ma Mite

From:	Mark Mitchell	To:	Bob Gibson
Sent:	12 February 2008 09:59	Subject:	Re: Curry

Ma – Any chance you can cook me a really nice piece of meat tonight?

T.Bone

From:	Bob Gibson	To:	Mark Mitchell
Sent:	12 February 2008 10:17	Subject:	Re: Curry

Would you like some pasta to go with that?

Lynne Gweeny

re: gardening

| **From:** | Mark Mitchell | **To:** | Bob Gibson |
| **Sent:** | 14 March 2008 12:01 | **Subject:** | Re: Gardening |

I do like shrubs in the garden.

Yours

Laurel

| **From:** | Bob Gibson | **To:** | Mark Mitchell |
| **Sent:** | 14 March 2008 12:07 | **Subject:** | Re: Gardening |

You do need to keep them looking tidy though.

Pru Ning

| **From:** | Mark Mitchell | **To:** | Bob Gibson |
| **Sent:** | 14 March 2008 12:11 | **Subject:** | Re: Gardening |

Yes, and the same goes for all the flowers.

Yours

Chris Anthemum

| **From:** | Bob Gibson | **To:** | Mark Mitchell |
| **Sent:** | 14 March 2008 12:15 | **Subject:** | Re: Gardening |

Don't let the sharp leaves cut your fingers though.

Yours

Holly Bushe

From:	Mark Mitchell	**To:**	Bob Gibson
Sent:	14 March 2008 12:19	**Subject:**	Re: Gardening

I've only got a small garden myself, so I collect flowers from up on the moors.

Heather

From:	Bob Gibson	**To:**	Mark Mitchell
Sent:	14 March 2008 12:29	**Subject:**	Re: Gardening

Nice to hear from you Heather. My main problem is getting rid of some of the weeds from my lawn.

Dan D'Lyon

From:	Mark Mitchell	**To:**	Bob Gibson
Sent:	14 March 2008 12:37	**Subject:**	Re: Gardening

Although I do find some of those small flowers on my lawn quite attractive.

Daisy

From:	Bob Gibson	**To:**	Mark Mitchell
Sent:	14 March 2008 12:39	**Subject:**	Re: Gardening

They are Daisy. It's just that I'm taking great care to ensure my garden is in top shape this summer.

Walter Regularly

From:	Mark Mitchell	To:	Bob Gibson
Sent:	14 March 2008 12:45	Subject:	Re: Gardening

I do the same as you, but I have very poor soil in my garden and nothing will grow efficiently.

Sandy

From:	Bob Gibson	To:	Mark Mitchell
Sent:	14 March 2008 12:51	Subject:	Re: Gardening

Sandy. Do what I do and put your soil through some kind of sieve.

Yours

Phil Terr

re: marriage

| **From:** | Mark Mitchell | **To:** | Bob Gibson |
| **Sent:** | 10 April 2008 09:38 | **Subject:** | Re: Marriage |

I'm getting married in the spring.

Yours

June Bride

| **From:** | Bob Gibson | **To:** | Mark Mitchell |
| **Sent:** | 10 April 2008 09:42 | **Subject:** | Re: Marriage |

Me too!

Yours

May Bride

| **From:** | Mark Mitchell | **To:** | Bob Gibson |
| **Sent:** | 10 April 2008 09:45 | **Subject:** | Re: Marriage |

Congratulations. I'm having second thoughts about getting hitched.

May Marry

| **From:** | Bob Gibson | **To:** | Mark Mitchell |
| **Sent:** | 10 April 2008 09:51 | **Subject:** | Re: Marriage |

I'm only doing it for the precious stone I got in my engagement ring.

Yours

Di Mond

From:	Mark Mitchell	To:	Bob Gibson
Sent:	10 April 2008 09:56	Subject:	Re: Marriage

Me too Di.

Emma Ruld

From:	Bob Gibson	To:	Mark Mitchell
Sent:	10 April 2008 10:00	Subject:	Re: Marriage

I'm not sure we're doing it for the right reasons. But a new gemstone is always appealing.

Ruby

From:	Mark Mitchell	To:	Bob Gibson
Sent:	10 April 2008 10:04	Subject:	Re: Marriage

Ruby. That's my second-favourite shade of red

Yours

Scarlett

From:	Bob Gibson	To:	Mark Mitchell
Sent:	10 April 2008 10:06	Subject:	Re: Marriage

All this talk reminds me that I haven't decided on what colour flowers to hold. I might have a variety.

Ray Bow

From:	Mark Mitchell	To:	Bob Gibson
Sent:	10 April 2008 10:09	Subject:	Re: Marriage

That sounds lovely. Make sure you throw them in my direction please!

Bo Kay

From:	Bob Gibson	To:	Mark Mitchell
Sent:	10 April 2008 10:38	Subject:	Re: Marriage

I'll be getting my flowers from the local supermarket.

Tess Coe

From:	Mark Mitchell	To:	Bob Gibson
Sent:	10 April 2008 10:45	Subject:	Re: Marriage

I could get a discount on mine; I've started a new job as a delivery driver.

Van Morrison

From:	Bob Gibson	To:	Mark Mitchell
Sent:	10 April 2008 10:54	Subject:	Re: Marriage

I bet I can get them even cheaper than you.

Al Dee

From:	Mark Mitchell	To:	Bob Gibson
Sent:	10 April 2008 10:57	Subject:	Re: Marriage

I do know how to get them for free, but please keep it to yourself.

Nick One

From:	Bob Gibson	To:	Mark Mitchell
Sent:	10 April 2008 11:01	Subject:	Re: Marriage

OK. I'll make sure you're invited to the wedding. Don't expect anything too modern, it will be a traditional church ceremony.

Cath O'Lick

From:	Mark Mitchell	To:	Bob Gibson
Sent:	10 April 2008 11:08	Subject:	Re: Marriage

Mine too.

Chris T. Anne

From:	Bob Gibson	To:	Mark Mitchell
Sent:	10 April 2008 11:11	Subject:	Re: Marriage

Hey Cath – I can recommend a great venue for your wedding if you're stuck.

Wes Minster-Abbey

From:	Mark Mitchell	To:	Bob Gibson
Sent:	10 April 2008 11:17	Subject:	Re: Marriage

Will you be greeting people before the main party gets underway?

Yours

Rhys Epshun

From:	Bob Gibson	To:	Mark Mitchell
Sent:	10 April 2008 12:02	Subject:	Re: Marriage

I will Rhys. And once the speeches are over we can start the music.

Dan Singh

From:	Mark Mitchell	To:	Bob Gibson
Sent:	10 April 2008 12:21	Subject:	Re: Marriage

Brilliant Dan. I'm really coming for the food. Will there be a menu that I can choose whatever I like from?

Alec Art

From:	Bob Gibson	To:	Mark Mitchell
Sent:	10 April 2008 12:31	Subject:	Re: Marriage

You can choose a dessert Alec, but the starters are already decided.

Mel On

| **From:** | Mark Mitchell | **To:** | Bob Gibson |
| **Sent:** | 10 April 2008 12:41 | **Subject:** | Re: Marriage |

Mel, is it a very formal party? Will I need to dress up?

Yours

Dickie Bow

| **From:** | Bob Gibson | **To:** | Mark Mitchell |
| **Sent:** | 10 April 2008 12:44 | **Subject:** | Re: Marriage |

No Dickie, it's not formal.

Fran C. Dress

| **From:** | Mark Mitchell | **To:** | Bob Gibson |
| **Sent:** | 10 April 2008 12:51 | **Subject:** | Re: Marriage |

In that case I may dress in a regency theme and travel in an appropriate mode of transport.

Yours

Orson Carriage

| **From:** | Bob Gibson | **To:** | Mark Mitchell |
| **Sent:** | 10 April 2008 12:57 | **Subject:** | Re: Marriage |

That's fine Orson. What do you prefer with your meal? Red or white? I'm ordering it in from Birmingham.

Y. Enn

| **From:** | Mark Mitchell | **To:** | Bob Gibson |
| **Sent:** | 10 April 2008 13:15 | **Subject:** | Re: Marriage |

I'll be happy with either, as long as we say a prayer before the meal.

Yours

Grace

| **From:** | Bob Gibson | **To:** | Mark Mitchell |
| **Sent:** | 10 April 2008 13:31 | **Subject:** | Re: Marriage |

We will Grace. I've already got someone lined up to take care of that.

Vic Are

| **From:** | Mark Mitchell | **To:** | Bob Gibson |
| **Sent:** | 10 April 2008 13:36 | **Subject:** | Re: Marriage |

Why, why, why couldn't that b@*tard turn up on our wedding day? He's ruined my life and made me look like such an idiot. I'll never forgive him.

Yours

Jill Tidd

re: army

From:	Mark Mitchell	To:	Bob Gibson
Sent:	05 May 2008 09:01	Subject:	Re: Army

I love my job in the army, but I do think they load my back pack with too many things.

Yours

Para Phernalia

From:	Bob Gibson	To:	Mark Mitchell
Sent:	05 May 2008 09:09	Subject:	Re: Army

I'm sorry to hear that Mr. Phernalia, but if it's too heavy you might want to get something to carry it all in. Like one of those snazzy army vehicles that work on land and sea.

Yours

Anne Phibious

From:	Mark Mitchell	To:	Bob Gibson
Sent:	05 May 2008 09:12	Subject:	Re: Army

That's true Anne. But on a more positive note just let me know when you want to take on the enemy – we're all ready.

Bette Allian

From:	Bob Gibson	To:	Mark Mitchell
Sent:	05 May 2008 09:16	Subject:	Re: Army

Will do. Hope we don't let our ancestors down. The allied forces did a fantastic job on D-Day.

Yours

Norman Dee

From:	Mark Mitchell	**To:**	Bob Gibson
Sent:	05 May 2008 09:31	**Subject:**	Re: Army

I'm laughing loud at that one Norm! It's great when we all stick together.

Al Ayed-Forces

From:	Bob Gibson	**To:**	Mark Mitchell
Sent:	05 May 2008 09:40	**Subject:**	Re: Army

They don't fight wars like they used to Al.

Norman Conquest

From:	Mark Mitchell	**To:**	Bob Gibson
Sent:	05 May 2008 09:45	**Subject:**	Re: Army

They didn't fight wars at all when I was a boy.

Jack O'Bean

From:	Bob Gibson	**To:**	Mark Mitchell
Sent:	05 May 2008 09:52	**Subject:**	Re: Army

I'm not a full time soldier Jack.
I just get involved occasionally; weekends & the like.

Yours

Terry Torial

From:	Mark Mitchell	To:	Bob Gibson
Sent:	05 May 2008 09:57	Subject:	Re: Army

Yes, but remember that armies march on their stomachs so don't forget to pack plenty of tasty, fizzy sweets.

Yours

Harry Bow

From:	Bob Gibson	To:	Mark Mitchell
Sent:	05 May 2008 10:02	Subject:	Re: Army

Thanks for the tip Harry. Keep it to yourself but I've actually pinched some of mum's chocolate.

Ma's Bar

From:	Mark Mitchell	To:	Bob Gibson
Sent:	05 May 2008 10:08	Subject:	Re: Army

I don't really care. I'm feeling quite depressed having been sent home from the front line after being hit by a bullet that bounced off a wall.

Yours

Rick O'Shay

re: building

From:	Mark Mitchell	To:	Bob Gibson
Sent:	08 May 2008 12:36	Subject:	Re: Building

Great photos of the house - did you get Den O'Lition to do the work? I thought you would have kept more garden space for the children to play in though.

Mr. Nopportunity

From:	Bob Gibson	To:	Mark Mitchell
Sent:	08 May 2008 12:40	Subject:	Re: Building

You could be right. It's not a problem now but it might be when they start walking.

Todd Lerr

From:	Mark Mitchell	To:	Bob Gibson
Sent:	08 May 2008 12:47	Subject:	Re: Building

Don't worry about it Todd – the stone fireplace you've built in the lounge will compensate. It's very impressive.

Yours

Sue Perb

From:	Bob Gibson	To:	Mark Mitchell
Sent:	08 May 2008 13:02	Subject:	Re: Building

Thanks for the compliment Sue. I've now commissioned someone to finish the house.

Bill Der

From:	Mark Mitchell	To:	Bob Gibson
Sent:	08 May 2008 13:09	Subject:	Re: Building

Nice one Bill. You'll need specialist help with some of the work - keep me in mind won't you.

Ruth

From:	Bob Gibson	To:	Mark Mitchell
Sent:	08 May 2008 13:15	Subject:	Re: Building

Will do Ruth, but please make sure you do a good job of it. If not I'll take you to court.

Sue

From:	Mark Mitchell	To:	Bob Gibson
Sent:	08 May 2008 13:18	Subject:	Re: Building

That's a bit aggressive Sue – surely there's a fairer solution.

R. Bitration

From:	Bob Gibson	To:	Mark Mitchell
Sent:	08 May 2008 13:24	Subject:	Re: Building

Well, I'll certainly need easy access to the garden from the lounge if you can help with that.

Paddy O'Dores

From:	Mark Mitchell	To:	Bob Gibson
Sent:	08 May 2008 13:26	Subject:	Re: Building

OK Paddy – I'll give you a call. Let me know if you need help with the woodwork too.

Joy Ner

From:	Bob Gibson	To:	Mark Mitchell
Sent:	08 May 2008 13:33	Subject:	Re: Building

Take care with those hammers Joy. I don't want to have to take you to A&E.

Oz Pital

From:	Mark Mitchell	To:	Bob Gibson
Sent:	08 May 2008 14:02	Subject:	Re: Building

No worries Oz – I'll be careful. It's more the problem of using a building site toilet that worries me.

Paul Taloo

From:	Bob Gibson	To:	Mark Mitchell
Sent:	08 May 2008 14:09	Subject:	Re: Building

Yes I understand Paul – they're not the most fragrant of places are they.

O. Durr

From:	Mark Mitchell	To:	Bob Gibson
Sent:	08 May 2008 14:15	Subject:	Re: Building

I prefer a good old-fashioned lavatory.

Yours

John

From:	Bob Gibson	To:	Mark Mitchell
Sent:	08 May 2008 14:22	Subject:	Re: Building

Just be careful with all this digging – if you damage too many roots you'll be in trouble.

Teresa Dying

From:	Mark Mitchell	To:	Bob Gibson
Sent:	08 May 2008 14:33	Subject:	Re: Building

I hope that doesn't happen. It's nice to have a garden surrounded by trees.

Woody

From:	Bob Gibson	To:	Mark Mitchell
Sent:	08 May 2008 14:44	Subject:	Re: Building

I'm with you there Woody. I'll be glad to help out with any planting.

A. Corn

From:	Mark Mitchell	To:	Bob Gibson
Sent:	08 May 2008 14:50	Subject:	Re: Building

If you're too busy with work to get those little jobs done, just get someone in to do them.

Yours

Andy Mann

From:	Bob Gibson	To:	Mark Mitchell
Sent:	08 May 2008 14:58	Subject:	Re: Building

Will do Andy. You know, I really don't like all our new furniture. I'd much rather have something with a bit of history attached to it.

Yours

Anne Teak

From:	Mark Mitchell	To:	Bob Gibson
Sent:	08 May 2008 15:15	Subject:	Re: Building

Nice one Anne. I'm particularly keen on old fashioned light fittings.

Yours

Candy Larborough

re: cakes

From:	Mark Mitchell	To:	Bob Gibson
Sent:	09 May 2008 16:50	Subject:	Re: Cakes

I didn't get chance to go to the canteen this morning.

Miss T. Break

From:	Bob Gibson	To:	Mark Mitchell
Sent:	09 May 2008 16:55	Subject:	Re: Cakes

Please get something for me if you do get chance for a break later. I'd love a piece of cake.

Yours

Victoria Sponge

From:	Mark Mitchell	To:	Bob Gibson
Sent:	09 May 2008 17:03	Subject:	Re: Cakes

I prefer biscuits myself.

Gary Baldy

From:	Bob Gibson	To:	Mark Mitchell
Sent:	09 May 2008 17:10	Subject:	Re: Cakes

Fantastic Gary! What a response! I love a wholewheat biscuit; not quite such a sin

Yours

Di Gestiv

From:	Mark Mitchell	To:	Bob Gibson
Sent:	09 May 2008 17:15	Subject:	Re: Cakes

Great one Di. I sometimes choose the healthier option too.

Yours

Hazel Nut

From:	Bob Gibson	To:	Mark Mitchell
Sent:	09 May 2008 17:21	Subject:	Re: Cakes

I knew you were going to say that Hazel.

Claire Voyant

From:	Mark Mitchell	To:	Bob Gibson
Sent:	09 May 2008 17:26	Subject:	Re: Cakes

You always come out with the the most enlightening lines Claire.

Pearl Sofwisdom

re: cycling

From:	Mark Mitchell	To:	Bob Gibson
Sent:	11 May 2008 14:30	Subject:	Re: Cycling

I can now cycle in the dark thanks to my new lights, they don't require batteries.

Yours

Di Namo

From:	Bob Gibson	To:	Mark Mitchell
Sent:	11 May 2008 14:34	Subject:	Re: Cycling

Don't forget to protect your head when you're out too.

Si Kelhelmet

From:	Mark Mitchell	To:	Bob Gibson
Sent:	11 May 2008 14:42	Subject:	Re: Cycling

Good advice Si, although I'm pretty sure people will hear me coming.

Belle

From:	Bob Gibson	To:	Mark Mitchell
Sent:	11 May 2008 14:45	Subject:	Re: Cycling

OK Belle, but please hold tight when you're cycling.

Anne D'Elbarrs

From:	Mark Mitchell	To:	Bob Gibson
Sent:	11 May 2008 14:52	Subject:	Re: Cycling

And don't forget your tool kit Anne.

Alan Quey

From:	Bob Gibson	To:	Mark Mitchell
Sent:	11 May 2008 14:56	Subject:	Re: Cycling

When I'm not out on my bike I get a lot of pleasure from gathering all my stamps in one book.

Yours

Al Bumm

From:	Mark Mitchell	To:	Bob Gibson
Sent:	11 May 2008 14:59	Subject:	Re: Cycling

I prefer tennis or squash, although I've got trouble with my arm now.

Yours

Elle Bow

re: camping

| **From:** | Mark Mitchell | **To:** | Bob Gibson |
| **Sent:** | 23 May 2008 12:36 | **Subject:** | Re: Camping |

Looking forward to our camping trip this weekend. I'll be driving down from Birmingham so could someone please provide a map or postcode for me.

Yours

Em Forty

| **From:** | Bob Gibson | **To:** | Mark Mitchell |
| **Sent:** | 23 May 2008 12:42 | **Subject:** | Re: Camping |

Will do. And in case it's windy I suggest you bring something to hold your tent down.

Yours

Guy Rope

| **From:** | Mark Mitchell | **To:** | Bob Gibson |
| **Sent:** | 23 May 2008 12:45 | **Subject:** | Re: Camping |

Do be careful though because too many ropes will mean a lot of hammering.

Yours

Peggy

| **From:** | Bob Gibson | **To:** | Mark Mitchell |
| **Sent:** | 23 May 2008 12:59 | **Subject:** | Re: Camping |

Nice one Peggy. I've just checked the weather forecast and it looks like there may be a little rain. I suggest you bring a lightweight waterproof jacket.

Yours

Anne O'Rack

From:	Mark Mitchell	To:	Bob Gibson
Sent:	23 May 2008 13:04	Subject:	Re: Camping

You're on top form Anne. If it does rain it will put our cooking plans out.

Barbara Queue

From:	Bob Gibson	To:	Mark Mitchell
Sent:	23 May 2008 13:08	Subject:	Re: Camping

That'd be a real shame as I love eating outdoors.

Yours

Alf Resco

From:	Mark Mitchell	To:	Bob Gibson
Sent:	23 May 2008 13:12	Subject:	Re: Camping

Especially breakfast Alf.

Chris P. Bacon

From:	Bob Gibson	To:	Mark Mitchell
Sent:	23 May 2008 13:15	Subject:	Re: Camping

I'll bring the gas rings – if it gets cold I'll warm up a tin of Heinz's finest.

Sue Oop

From:	Mark Mitchell	**To:**	Bob Gibson
Sent:	23 May 2008 13:19	**Subject:**	Re: Camping

Great, I really like soup.

Yours

Minnie Stroney

From:	Bob Gibson	**To:**	Mark Mitchell
Sent:	23 May 2008 13:27	**Subject:**	Re: Camping

Great one Minnie.
Not my favourite though.

Lee Kandpotatoe

From:	Mark Mitchell	**To:**	Bob Gibson
Sent:	23 May 2008 13:33	**Subject:**	Re: Camping

Good one Lee – I've now found out where we will be driving to.

Yours

Henry On-Thames (Esq.)

From:	Bob Gibson	**To:**	Mark Mitchell
Sent:	23 May 2008 13:41	**Subject:**	Re: Camping

Excellent Henry. Please be aware that there's a fishing lake at the campsite so come prepared.

Yours

Rod

From:	Mark Mitchell	**To:**	Bob Gibson
Sent:	23 May 2008 13:47	**Subject:**	Re: Camping

Well done Rod – do you know if you have to pay to fish?

Yours

Bill

From:	Bob Gibson	**To:**	Mark Mitchell
Sent:	23 May 2008 13:52	**Subject:**	Re: Camping

Not sure Bill. It's looking a bit wet out there!

Yours

Ray Knee

From:	Mark Mitchell	**To:**	Bob Gibson
Sent:	23 May 2008 13:57	**Subject:**	Re: Camping

Thanks Ray – you are on form today. I'm planning on bringing our kite but that depends on the weather.

Wendy Day

From:	Bob Gibson	**To:**	Mark Mitchell
Sent:	23 May 2008 13:59	**Subject:**	Re: Camping

It's a shame we only do it once a year.

Regards

Anne Uley

Great to see you all camping this weekend, good to catch up. I can hardly wait 'til next year. But I guess I'll just have to.

Yours

Anne Ticipation

re: Kids' books

From:	Mark Mitchell	To:	Bob Gibson
Sent:	20 June 2008 16:08	Subject:	Re: Kid's Books

I love Gulliver's Travels.

Yours

Lily Putt

From:	Bob Gibson	To:	Mark Mitchell
Sent:	20 June 2008 16:11	Subject:	Re: Kid's Books

Me too Lily. In fact I love all children's stories.

Faye Muss-Five

From:	Mark Mitchell	To:	Bob Gibson
Sent:	20 June 2008 16:18	Subject:	Re: Kid's Books

Excellent one Faye. I'm a big fan of J.M. Barrie myself.

Yours

Nev Erland

From:	Bob Gibson	To:	Mark Mitchell
Sent:	20 June 2008 16:24	Subject:	Re: Kid's Books

Nev – that's ace. But I still prefer Enid Blyton's novels.

C. Cretseven

From:	Mark Mitchell	To:	Bob Gibson
Sent:	20 June 2008 16:29 .	Subject:	Re: Kid's Books

I generally like any story which has a hidden lesson in it.

Yours

Faye Ball

From:	Bob Gibson	To:	Mark Mitchell
Sent:	20 June 2008 16:33	Subject:	Re: Kid's Books

I'm with you there.

E. Sopp

From:	Mark Mitchell	To:	Bob Gibson
Sent:	20 June 2008 16:39	Subject:	Re: Kid's Books

To be honest, any story would do for me.

Jackie Norey

From:	Bob Gibson	To:	Mark Mitchell
Sent:	20 June 2008 16:55	Subject:	Re: Kid's Books

I don't really care what my bedtime story is – just as long as I have something to cuddle.

Ted

re: FUN Fair

From:	Mark Mitchell	To:	Bob Gibson
Sent:	08 July 2008 10:41	Subject:	Re: Fun Fair

I'm going to the seaside today – can you meet me in the evening at about 8pm?

Pierre End

From:	Bob Gibson	To:	Mark Mitchell
Sent:	08 July 2008 10:49	Subject:	Re: Fun Fair

OK Pierre but don't go on about it if I'm late

E.R. Ache

From:	Mark Mitchell	To:	Bob Gibson
Sent:	08 July 2008 10:51	Subject:	Re: Fun Fair

Oh he does go on about it, and I've had enough of it, always complaining, always rabbitting on – it gets very tiring.

Mo Ning

From:	Bob Gibson	To:	Mark Mitchell
Sent:	08 July 2008 10:55	Subject:	Re: Fun Fair

Cheer up all of you – get down to the fun fair and enjoy yourselves.

Yours

Mary Goround

I will go Mary. But only if you'll buy me a treat.

Candy Floss

re: iLLness

From:	Mark Mitchell	To:	Bob Gibson
Sent:	09 July 2008 08:57	Subject:	Re: Illness

My back's playing up.

Si Attica

From:	Bob Gibson	To:	Mark Mitchell
Sent:	09 July 2008 09:14	Subject:	Re: Illness

Sorry to hear that Si. I've not been feeling too good myself lately.

Yours

Paul Lee

From:	Mark Mitchell	To:	Bob Gibson
Sent:	09 July 2008 09:17	Subject:	Re: Illness

Great one Paul! I think I'm over the worst of it now.

Bette Terr

From:	Bob Gibson	To:	Mark Mitchell
Sent:	09 July 2008 09:20	Subject:	Re: Illness

Me too – throat's still a bit sore though.

Larry N. Jituss

From:	Mark Mitchell	To:	Bob Gibson
Sent:	09 July 2008 09:24	Subject:	Re: Illness

I'm feeling sick now Larry.

Yours

Nora Virus

From:	Bob Gibson	To:	Mark Mitchell
Sent:	09 July 2008 09:33	Subject:	Re: Illness

Oscar's not been well at all, but we're managing to treat it with some great medicine.

Yours

Benny Lynn

From:	Mark Mitchell	To:	Bob Gibson
Sent:	09 July 2008 09:56	Subject:	Re: Illness

Benny – I wish that would work for me. My legs are so sore I can't even stand up.

Neil

From:	Bob Gibson	To:	Mark Mitchell
Sent:	09 July 2008 10:14	Subject:	Re: Illness

You need to be careful with your joints – you could get long term damage.

Arthur Rytis

From:	Mark Mitchell	To:	Bob Gibson
Sent:	09 July 2008 10:45	Subject:	Re: Illness

Thanks for the tip Arthur. I'm not too worried to be honest as I understand they can inject fluid into you joints these days to loosen things up.

Lou Bricant

From:	Bob Gibson	To:	Mark Mitchell
Sent:	09 July 2008 11:10	Subject:	Re: Illness

On top of all that I've been very depressed lately, so the doctor's prescribed some serious medication for me.

Yours

Val Ium

From:	Mark Mitchell	To:	Bob Gibson
Sent:	09 July 2008 11:17	Subject:	Re: Illness

Sorry to hear you've not been yourself recently Val. I've had tonsillitis and the doc's given me some great tablets.

Yours

Penny Silyn

From:	Bob Gibson	To:	Mark Mitchell
Sent:	09 July 2008 11:28	Subject:	Re: Illness

Hi Penny. Glad to hear that you're back on form. I try to avoid being poorly in the first place by relaxing in a warm bubble-bath.

Yours

Ray Dox

From:	Mark Mitchell	To:	Bob Gibson
Sent:	09 July 2008 11:55	Subject:	Re: Illness

Good idea Ray. While you're at it you should use a mild shampoo to wash your hair.

Yours

Tim O'Tay

From:	Bob Gibson	To:	Mark Mitchell
Sent:	09 July 2008 11:59	Subject:	Re: Illness

I've just bought an enormous bath which I plan to relax in tonight. It's so deep I can't even touch the bottom.

Bob Uppendown

re: marketing

| **From:** | Mark Mitchell | **To:** | Bob Gibson |
| **Sent:** | 23 July 2008 15:07 | **Subject:** | Re: Marketing |

How's the job going? I'm just drawing up some informative illustrations for a text book.

Di Agram

| **From:** | Bob Gibson | **To:** | Mark Mitchell |
| **Sent:** | 23 July 2008 15:11 | **Subject:** | Re: Marketing |

Job's going well thanks Di. Flat out at the moment though.

B. Zee

| **From:** | Mark Mitchell | **To:** | Bob Gibson |
| **Sent:** | 23 July 2008 15:17 | **Subject:** | Re: Marketing |

Good to hear it Mr Zee. I'm trying to get some more work in at the moment, advertising & that sort of thing.

Mark Ettin

| **From:** | Bob Gibson | **To:** | Mark Mitchell |
| **Sent:** | 23 July 2008 15:29 | **Subject:** | Re: Marketing |

Excellent Mark. I prefer to specialise.

Di Rect-Mail

From:	Mark Mitchell	To:	Bob Gibson
Sent:	23 July 2008 15:33	Subject:	Re: Marketing

I like your thinking. I may try some letterbox drops.

Yours

Lee Flets

From:	Bob Gibson	To:	Mark Mitchell
Sent:	23 July 2008 15:46	Subject:	Re: Marketing

Lee – that's superb! You may find that you have more success with a direct approach.

Tel E. Sales

From:	Mark Mitchell	To:	Bob Gibson
Sent:	23 July 2008 15:59	Subject:	Re: Marketing

Give me a couple of lines on what you can / can't do; I have a great contact who I'll call for you in the meantime.

Yours

Nat Working

From:	Bob Gibson	To:	Mark Mitchell
Sent:	23 July 2008 16:07	Subject:	Re: Marketing

I think I'd prefer to advertise with a local broadcaster.

Yours

Ray Deo

From:	Mark Mitchell	To:	Bob Gibson
Sent:	23 July 2008 16:21	Subject:	Re: Marketing

Dial 0800 800 800 now!

Michael Tooaction

From:	Bob Gibson	To:	Mark Mitchell
Sent:	23 July 2008 16:28	Subject:	Re: Marketing

Hi Michael, me again. I'm still struggling to get my message across.

Yours

Miss Communicate

From:	Mark Mitchell	To:	Bob Gibson
Sent:	23 July 2008 16:38	Subject:	Re: Marketing

If you're struggling why don't you dress up as a bear and run the London Marathon?

P.R. Stunt

From:	Bob Gibson	To:	Mark Mitchell
Sent:	23 July 2008 16:44	Subject:	Re: Marketing

Could do – I'm sure I've got some photos from last year's race on my PC.

Yours

R. Kive

From:	Mark Mitchell	To:	Bob Gibson
Sent:	23 July 2008 16:49	Subject:	Re: Marketing

Great, could you forward them to my laptop?

Mack

chapter 16

re: scandinavia

From:	Mark Mitchell	To:	Bob Gibson
Sent:	13 August 2008 08:37	Subject:	Re: Scandinavia

I love living in Northern Europe.

Finn Land

From:	Bob Gibson	To:	Mark Mitchell
Sent:	13 August 2008 09.32	Subject:	Re: Scandinavia

I do too Finn – it's the winter sports that appeal.

Dawn Hillskier

From:	Mark Mitchell	To:	Bob Gibson
Sent:	13 August 2008 09.41	Subject:	Re: Scandinavia

I like winter sports too Dawn, but I'm more of a team player myself.

I. Sockey

From:	Bob Gibson	To:	Mark Mitchell
Sent:	13 August 2008 09.49	Subject:	Re: Scandinavia

Me too, I play that in my spare time – when I'm not performing in A Midsummer Night's Dream.

Puck

From:	Mark Mitchell	**To:**	Bob Gibson
Sent:	13 August 2008 09.55	**Subject:**	Re: Scandanavia

Puck! What sort of a name is that? You're living in the olden days.

Liz E. Beethan

From:	Bob Gibson	**To:**	Mark Mitchell
Sent:	13 August 2008 10:17	**Subject:**	Re: Scandinavia

Nothing wrong with the olden days Liz – I'm very fond of them.

George Anne

From:	Mark Mitchell	**To:**	Bob Gibson
Sent:	13 August 2008 10:21	**Subject:**	Re: Scandinavia

You need to get a bit more up to date.

A. Tees

From:	Bob Gibson	**To:**	Mark Mitchell
Sent:	13 August 2008 10:27	**Subject:**	Re: Scandinavia

Why stop there Miss Tees? You should plan way ahead if you ask me.

Frew Turistic

re: travel

From:	Mark Mitchell	To:	Bob Gibson
Sent:	25 August 2008 14:08	Subject:	Re: Travel

Hi, did you go anywhere nice on your hols? We managed to get to Turkey.

Yours

Anne Karra

From:	Bob Gibson	To:	Mark Mitchell
Sent:	25 August 2008 14:11	Subject:	Re: Travel

Good one Anne – we went to a resort in Tenerife.

Chris T. Arnos

From:	Mark Mitchell	To:	Bob Gibson
Sent:	25 August 2008 14:14	Subject:	Re: Travel

We're hoping to visit a US desert next year.

Yours

Harry Zona

From:	Bob Gibson	To:	Mark Mitchell
Sent:	25 August 2008 14:17	Subject:	Re: Travel

Good effort Harry – I'm heading for US sunshine too.

Flo Reeder

From:	Mark Mitchell	To:	Bob Gibson
Sent:	25 August 2008 14:20	Subject:	Re: Travel

There's a lot to take in over in the US. I'm hoping to get to the West Coast soon.

Yours

Callie Fornia

From:	Bob Gibson	To:	Mark Mitchell
Sent:	25 August 2008 14:23	Subject:	Re: Travel

Like it Callie. I'll come and see you (stopping off on the way).

Al B. Kerrkee

From:	Mark Mitchell	To:	Bob Gibson
Sent:	25 August 2008 14:26	Subject:	Re: Travel

Nice one Al. I'm sure there are better places to stop off.

Yours

Phil A. Delfia

From:	Bob Gibson	To:	Mark Mitchell
Sent:	25 August 2008 14:29	Subject:	Re: Travel

You'll be close to my home state there.

Penny Silvania

From:	Mark Mitchell	To:	Bob Gibson
Sent:	25 August 2008 14:33	Subject:	Re: Travel

Maybe I'll head North West instead.

Mary Land

From:	Bob Gibson	To:	Mark Mitchell
Sent:	25 August 2008 14:37	Subject:	Re: Travel

Oh there's plenty to go at in the States.

Yours

Mick Shigin

From:	Mark Mitchell	To:	Bob Gibson
Sent:	25 August 2008 14:41	Subject:	Re: Travel

Ever considered simply taking the ferry to Ireland?

Ross Lair

From:	Bob Gibson	To:	Mark Mitchell
Sent:	25 August 2008 14:45	Subject:	Re: Travel

No - flying long haul this year.

Ken Yah

| **From:** | Mark Mitchell | **To:** | Bob Gibson |
| **Sent:** | 25 August 2008 14:48 | **Subject:** | Re: Travel |

Oh superb Ken. Perhaps go via England's famous East coast?

Lou E. Stoft

| **From:** | Bob Gibson | **To:** | Mark Mitchell |
| **Sent:** | 25 August 2008 14:55 | **Subject:** | Re: Travel |

No, I prefer to head south to one of the most beautiful counties.

A. Vaughan

| **From:** | Mark Mitchell | **To:** | Bob Gibson |
| **Sent:** | 25 August 2008 15:03 | **Subject:** | Re: Travel |

Excellent Mr. Vaughan – though I do think it's good to head north.

Carl Isle

| **From:** | Bob Gibson | **To:** | Mark Mitchell |
| **Sent:** | 25 August 2008 15:08 | **Subject:** | Re: Travel |

I'd love to find a ski resort where the booze is tax free.

Yours

Anne Dora

From:	Mark Mitchell	To:	Bob Gibson
Sent:	25 August 2008 15:12	Subject:	Re: Travel

Or you could fly directly to Lanzarote Airport for some winter sun.

Harry C. Fay

From:	Bob Gibson	To:	Mark Mitchell
Sent:	25 August 2008 15:18	Subject:	Re: Travel

Good idea Harry – though I prefer to prolong my youth with my holiday choices.

Yours

Benny Dorm

From:	Mark Mitchell	To:	Bob Gibson
Sent:	25 August 2008 15:22	Subject:	Re: Travel

Nice one Benny. Good choice to go inland too, I hear some freak waves are due to hit the coast.

Yours

Sue Narmi

From:	Bob Gibson	To:	Mark Mitchell
Sent:	25 August 2008 15:27	Subject:	Re: Travel

I'm thinking of going on a European touring holiday this summer.

Benny Lux

From:	Mark Mitchell	To:	Bob Gibson
Sent:	25 August 2008 15:33	Subject:	Re: Travel

I'm thinking of taking a mid-year break next year.

Yours

June Holiday

From:	Bob Gibson	To:	Mark Mitchell
Sent:	25 August 2008 15:37	Subject:	Re: Travel

Nice one June. I've been considering a break myself but much longer term.

Yours

Seb Atical

From:	Mark Mitchell	To:	Bob Gibson
Sent:	25 August 2008 15:41	Subject:	Re: Travel

Come and see me first – I've moved to a place just outside Bromsgrove

Lydia Tash

From:	Bob Gibson	To:	Mark Mitchell
Sent:	25 August 2008 15:45	Subject:	Re: Travel

Why not look for a holiday in Portugal instead - you could take in a football game.

Yours

Ben Fica

From:	Mark Mitchell	To:	Bob Gibson
Sent:	25 August 2008 15:49	Subject:	Re: Travel

I prefer cruising myself.

O. Shun-Waves

From:	Bob Gibson	To:	Mark Mitchell
Sent:	25 August 2008 15:53	Subject:	Re: Travel

Let me know when you take your next trip Mr Shun-Waves, you should call in to see me.

I. Land.

From:	Mark Mitchell	To:	Bob Gibson
Sent:	25 August 2008 15:56	Subject:	Re: Travel

Mr. Land – we'd be delighted. Will it be okay to bring my mum to look after the kids?

Gran Canaria

From:	Bob Gibson	To:	Mark Mitchell
Sent:	25 August 2008 15:59	Subject:	Re: Travel

She'd be very welcome but you must warn her that there can be a lot of hot water vapour in the air.

Hugh Midity

re: workload

| **From:** | Mark Mitchell | **To:** | Bob Gibson |
| **Sent:** | 25 September 2008 08:37 | **Subject:** | Re: Workload |

I'm determined to get everything done today.

Helen Highwater

| **From:** | Bob Gibson | **To:** | Mark Mitchell |
| **Sent:** | 25 September 2008 08:45 | **Subject:** | Re: Workload |

That is a fantastic one Helen! Though I'm not too worried if I don't get things done today.

Yours

Lee Vitiltomorrow

| **From:** | Mark Mitchell | **To:** | Bob Gibson |
| **Sent:** | 25 September 2008 09:07 | **Subject:** | Re: Workload |

You need to make sure you leave time for a pint in your favouite boozer on the way home too.

Orson Jockey

| **From:** | Bob Gibson | **To:** | Mark Mitchell |
| **Sent:** | 25 September 2008 09:11 | **Subject:** | Re: Workload |

If you need extra energy to get things done my grandmother recommends eating sugar.

Yours

Gran U. Lated

From:	Mark Mitchell	**To:**	Bob Gibson
Sent:	25 September 2008 09:13	**Subject:**	Re: Workload

Extra energy is just what I need. I had a few too many last night.

Martin E. Cocktails

From:	Bob Gibson	**To:**	Mark Mitchell
Sent:	25 September 2008 09:17	**Subject:**	Re: Workload

I tend to avoid the booze these days. My vices lie in cheap sweets.

Yours

Penny Choo

From:	Mark Mitchell	**To:**	Bob Gibson
Sent:	25 September 2008 09:30	**Subject:**	Re: Workload

Excellent Penny – you must be running out of new names by now though.

Kenny Thinkofmore

From:	Bob Gibson	**To:**	Mark Mitchell
Sent:	25 September 2008 09:33	**Subject:**	Re: Workload

That was a bit of a dead-end for me. I asked all my colleagues if they could think of something but they couldn't either.

Adam Stumped

| From: | Mark Mitchell | To: | Bob Gibson |
| Sent: | 25 September 2008 09:40 | Subject: | Re: Workload |

I wouldn't trust your friend for a moment.

Eliza Lott

| From: | Bob Gibson | To: | Mark Mitchell |
| Sent: | 25 September 2008 09:41 | Subject: | Re: Workload |

He's not that bad. Some of what he says is true.

Eliza Little

| From: | Mark Mitchell | To: | Bob Gibson |
| Sent: | 25 September 2008 09:44 | Subject: | Re: Workload |

He also likes the sound of his own voice.

Mike Rowfone

| From: | Bob Gibson | To: | Mark Mitchell |
| Sent: | 25 September 2008 10:14 | Subject: | Re: Workload |

I've heard he gets a lot of unwelcome interference from his wife.

Fi D'Bak

From:	Mark Mitchell	To:	Bob Gibson
Sent:	25 September 2008 11.12	Subject:	Re: Workload

Yep – interference comes from everywhere

Ray D. O'Waves.

From:	Bob Gibson	To:	Mark Mitchell
Sent:	25 September 2008 11.35	Subject:	Re: Workload

If all this technology's doing your head in get out of the office and into the fresh air, but watch out for any bad weather.

Yours

Wayne Cloud

re: police

From:	Mark Mitchell	To:	Bob Gibson
Sent:	03 November 2008 14:02	Subject:	Re: Police

Thanks for the offer but I won't need a lift tonight. I'll drive.

Mike Arr

From:	Bob Gibson	To:	Mark Mitchell
Sent:	03 November 2008 14:07	Subject:	Re: Police

Drive carefully. The police can easily track you down if you're caught on camera.

Reg

From:	Mark Mitchell	To:	Bob Gibson
Sent:	03 November 2008 14:11	Subject:	Re: Police

Good tip Reg. I'm always on the look out for drivers breaking the law.

C.C. Teevee

From:	Bob Gibson	To:	Mark Mitchell
Sent:	03 November 2008 14:19	Subject:	Re: Police

It's like Big Brother with you around! How times have changed since my day.

P. Lerr

From:	Mark Mitchell	To:	Bob Gibson
Sent:	03 November 2008 14:24	Subject:	Re: Police

It was different in my day too Mr. Lerr.

Bobby

From:	Bob Gibson	To:	Mark Mitchell
Sent:	03 November 2008 14:30	Subject:	Re: Police

We all need more specialist policing these days.

Dee Tective

From:	Mark Mitchell	To:	Bob Gibson
Sent:	03 November 2008 14:33	Subject:	Re: Police

Where are you based these days Dee? I'm at head office now.

Scott Landyard

From:	Bob Gibson	To:	Mark Mitchell
Sent:	03 November 2008 14:35	Subject:	Re: Police

It's nice there isn't it Scott. Although I understand you have to have a certain profession before they'll let you in.

Paul Easeman

From:	Mark Mitchell	To:	Bob Gibson
Sent:	03 November 2008 14:38	Subject:	Re: Police

You do Paul – but if you progress then your career can really take off. The sky's the limit.

L.E. Copter

From:	Bob Gibson	To:	Mark Mitchell
Sent:	03 November 2008 14:44	Subject:	Re: Police

Or you can work with dogs if you choose.

Anne d'Lerr

From:	Mark Mitchell	To:	Bob Gibson
Sent:	03 November 2008 14:48	Subject:	Re: Police

I prefer being in the patrol car. I like to let people know I'm coming.

Si Wren

From:	Bob Gibson	To:	Mark Mitchell
Sent:	03 November 2008 14:57	Subject:	Re: Police

It's useful at times Si – but I prefer to catch criminals unawares.

Dawn Raids

re: this time next year

| **From:** | Mark Mitchell | **To:** | Bob Gibson |
| **Sent:** | 12 December 2008 07:55 | **Subject:** | Re: This Time Next Year |

Did you check to see how many signatures we've now got?

Yours

Count Names

| **From:** | Bob Gibson | **To:** | Mark Mitchell |
| **Sent:** | 12 December 2008 07:58 | **Subject:** | Re: This Time Next Year |

There are loads Count. Once we get this book published we're going to be rich, rich, rich.

Yours

Millie Onayre

| **From:** | Mark Mitchell | **To:** | Bob Gibson |
| **Sent:** | 12 December 2008 08:10 | **Subject:** | Re: This Time Next Year |

If this book takes off we could start writing another. Then another. Then another.

Billy Onayre

| **From:** | Bob Gibson | **To:** | Mark Mitchell |
| **Sent:** | 12 December 2008 08:13 | **Subject:** | Re: This Time Next Year |

I know. But let's stop messing around now we need to take this project more seriously.

Earnest

From:	Mark Mitchell	To:	Bob Gibson
Sent:	12 December 2008 08:17	Subject:	Re: This Time Next Year

Funny how the girls were "poo-pooing" this a couple of years ago and now, when there's the chance of buying a new frock from the proceeds, they're right behind us.

I feel like Einstein

Jean E. Uss

From:	Bob Gibson	To:	Mark Mitchell
Sent:	12 December 2008 08:21	Subject:	Re: This Time Next Year

Thanks Jean. By the way, I had to get up at 5.30am this morning to sign some books.

Yours

Earl E. Byrd

From:	Mark Mitchell	To:	Bob Gibson
Sent:	12 December 2008 08:25	Subject:	Re: This Time Next Year

Sorry to hear that Earl. My wife thinks we should have a launch party. Not sure where we could go though.

Ivy Restaurant

From:	Bob Gibson	To:	Mark Mitchell
Sent:	12 December 2008 08:28	Subject:	Re: This Time Next Year

Sounds good Ivy – what fonts do you think we should use?

R.E.L. Narrow

| **From:** | Mark Mitchell | **To:** | Bob Gibson |
| **Sent:** | 12 December 2008 08:33 | **Subject:** | Re: This Time Next Year |

Not sure but I think we'll get a great title – I'll get my thinking cap on.

A. Milliner

| **From:** | Bob Gibson | **To:** | Mark Mitchell |
| **Sent:** | 12 December 2008 08:38 | **Subject:** | Re: This Time Next Year |

I was working on a spreadsheet earlier but got waylaid with thoughts of book signing ceremonies.

Alf Inishit-Later

| **From:** | Mark Mitchell | **To:** | Bob Gibson |
| **Sent:** | 12 December 2008 08:42 | **Subject:** | Re: This Time Next Year |

Just checked the letterbox - no book signing contract there yet. Will speak in a few hours. I've set a reminder...

Al Armclock

| **From:** | Bob Gibson | **To:** | Mark Mitchell |
| **Sent:** | 12 December 2008 08:55 | **Subject:** | Re: This Time Next Year |

I'm not going to set all my hopes on this book making us rich. I may try other forms of money making too. Well - you never know - it could be me!

Lotty Ree

| **From:** | Mark Mitchell | **To:** | Bob Gibson |
| **Sent:** | 12 December 2008 08:59 | **Subject:** | Re: This Time Next Year |

You know you can do that on-line now but make sure your computer's up to date.

Yours

P.C. World

| **From:** | Bob Gibson | **To:** | Mark Mitchell |
| **Sent:** | 12 December 2008 09:15 | **Subject:** | Re: This Time Next Year |

If you're getting your old computer checked over get them to take a look at the smaller components too.

Mike Rowchip & Sir Kitboard

| **From:** | Mark Mitchell | **To:** | Bob Gibson |
| **Sent:** | 12 December 2008 09:18 | **Subject:** | Re: This Time Next Year |

Mike, I found some old emails and the content is very good.

Si Burr-Signatures

| **From:** | Bob Gibson | **To:** | Mark Mitchell |
| **Sent:** | 12 December 2008 09:25 | **Subject:** | Re: This Time Next Year |

Don't start spending your millions before you've cashed the cheque and paid it into the bank.

Rick C. Business

From:	Mark Mitchell	To:	Bob Gibson
Sent:	12 December 2008 09:31	Subject:	Re: This Time Next Year

Don't worry Rick – I wouldn't know where to start spending my money. I'm new to this game.

Deb U. Tant

From:	Bob Gibson	To:	Mark Mitchell
Sent:	12 December 2008 09:36	Subject:	Re: This Time Next Year

My advice is to wait a little while before you decide how to spend it.

Luke B. Foryouleap

From:	Mark Mitchell	To:	Bob Gibson
Sent:	12 December 2008 09:39	Subject:	Re: This Time Next Year

The first thing I'm going to do with the money is buy a new phone system for my car.

Hans Free

From:	Bob Gibson	To:	Mark Mitchell
Sent:	12 December 2008 09:44	Subject:	Re: This Time Next Year

Always good to be within the law Hans. Is your phone digital or the other kind?

Yours

Anna Logg

| **From:** | Mark Mitchell | **To:** | Bob Gibson |
| **Sent:** | 12 December 2008 09:49 | **Subject:** | Re: This Time Next Year |

Good point Anna – I'll check. That reminds me, the old goggle-box goes digital in a few weeks time.

Yours

Terry Vision

| **From:** | Bob Gibson | **To:** | Mark Mitchell |
| **Sent:** | 12 December 2008 09:54 | **Subject:** | Re: This Time Next Year |

You didn't have to remind me Terry. I'm all prepared and I've got myself an extra set top box just to be on the safe side. Well you never know...

Yours

Justin Case

| **From:** | Mark Mitchell | **To:** | Bob Gibson |
| **Sent:** | 12 December 2008 09:59 | **Subject:** | Re: This Time Next Year |

I'd take the risk of using the phone in my car – I don't have far to travel to work.

Yours

Mini Commute

| **From:** | Bob Gibson | **To:** | Mark Mitchell |
| **Sent:** | 12 December 2008 10:04 | **Subject:** | Re: This Time Next Year |

That's not very sensible Minnie – a group of us are going out for a few drinks after work on Friday. I'm staying sober though.

Yours

Will Drive

From:	Mark Mitchell	**To:**	Bob Gibson
Sent:	12 December 2008 10:11	**Subject:**	Re: This Time Next Year

Don't forget to pick me up Will (the usual place) and don't tell your wife.

Dolly Byrd

From:	Bob Gibson	**To:**	Mark Mitchell
Sent:	12 December 2008 10.14	**Subject:**	Re: This Time Next Year

I've heard that before!

Poppy Cock

From:	Mark Mitchell	**To:**	Bob Gibson
Sent:	12 December 2008 10:18	**Subject:**	Re: This Time Next Year

I know. By the way I see you're attending next month's conference.

Del E. Gate-List

From:	Bob Gibson	**To:**	Mark Mitchell
Sent:	12 December 2008 10:36	**Subject:**	Re: This Time Next Year

With all my royalties I'm going to buy a boat. Firstly though I've got to find some way of ensuring it doesn't drift away.

Yours

Anne Core

9 781904 312499